# FUTURE READY SCHOOL

## 10 PROVEN STRATEGIES FOR IMPLEMENTING **STEM** SUCCESSFULLY

# FUTURE  READY SCHOOL

## 10 PROVEN STRATEGIES FOR IMPLEMENTING **STEM** SUCCESSFULLY

Chetanya Sahu

Worldwide Published by

**Pendown** Press

**PENDOWN PRESS LLP**

An ISO 9001 & ISO 14001 Certified Co.,

**Regd. Office:** 3767A, Kanhaiya Nagar,

Tri Nagar, Delhi-110035

**Ph.:** 8130886000, 9650072927

**E-mail:** info@pendownpress.com

**Branch Office:** 1A/2A, 20, Hari Sadan, Ansari Road,

Daryaganj, New Delhi-110002

**Ph.:** 011-45794768

**Website:** PendownPress.com

**Edition:** 2024

**Price:** ₹ 299

**ISBN:** 978-93-6338-646-4



*Layout and Cover Designed by* Pendown Graphics Team
*Printed and Bound in India by* Thomson Press India Ltd.

*This book is dedicated to all progressive schools that can make a real change by fostering creativity, championing innovation, and nurturing the growth of students in today's ever-changing world.*

*Your commitment to shaping the future inspires us all!*

# Table of Contents

# *Acknowledgements*

I want to say a big thank you all for allowing me to share my experiences and insights with you. This book is the culmination of years of hard work, learning, and growth. I hope the words within these pages of this boo will inspire and guide you on your own journey of innovation.

First and foremost, I am deeply thankful to God, my Shivbaba, whose strength, knowledge, and wisdom have been the cornerstone in my journey, guiding me to achieve my goals.

I feel indebted to my parents and family who have always stood by me like a rock. Your unwavering love, patience, and encouragement has made this endeavor possible.

My sincere gratitude towards my mentors and teachers, who provided me a strong foundation and to my incredible team at ABL Education – you are my pillars of strength, supporting and fueling this vision of mine. Last but not the least to the inspiring community of learned educators around me. Your guidance and collaboration have been invaluable in my growth.

A special thanks to my friend, Dinesh Verma, CEO of Pendown Press, and his team for their constant support and help throughout this journey.

To everyone mentioned here – and to those whose names may not have appear but whose contributions are deeply felt. Thank you for being a part of this journey! Together, we have created something truly special. I feel looking forward a journey of a thousand miles begins from here for me!

Thank you for being a part of this experience!

*With gratitude and warmth,*

*Chetanya Sahu*

# *Preface*

Education is a dynamic and an ever-evolving field. In order to truly prepare students for the future, our approach to learning must evolve. This book is for all the progressive schools— that welcome new ideas and innovations, embrace change, and are committed to equipping students for a world that's advancing at an unprecedented pace.

It's about creating environments where students don't just memorize facts but develop the skills to think critically, solve real-world problems, and collaborate effectively. These are the skills that will empower them to thrive in a future full of both challenges and opportunities.

Over the years, I've realized that success in today's world requires moving beyond traditional methods. Education must adapt and evolve. This book explores how schools can navigate this transformation, using forward-thinking approaches like STEM education to make learning more engaging, hands-on, and relevant to a students' life. It highlights the importance of nurturing both students and educators, providing them with the tools, opportunities, and inspiration they need for growth.

Within these pages, you'll discover insights, practical strategies, and real-life examples to help transform your school into a hub of creativity, innovation, and curiosity. Whether you're a school leader, teacher, or an advocate for better education, my hope is that this book will ignite a passion for creating a learning environment that truly prepares students for the future.

Together, let's reimagine education as a source of excitement and inspiration for both students and teachers—preparing the next generation to face tomorrow's world with confidence, creativity, and a love for learning.

# Foreword

There is a tremendous need for rapid transformation in approaches and methodologies related to STEM-based school education, factoring in the rapid technological changes that are happening in the world today.

These changes demand a fresh approach to teaching methods and the integration of practical experimentation in STEM for young school students in a very creative manner.

Chetanya Sahu, through his extraordinary interactions with school leaders, teachers, and students, comprehensively brings out, in an easily readable manner, the new strategies that need to be adopted, aligned with the National Education Policy, NEP 2020.

Chetanya is keen to ensure that the students of today become the problem solvers of tomorrow. The book articulates strategies that are practical to implement and yet impactful in their outcomes.

This book is an important tool for anyone who is keen to ensure a creative, implementable approach to the above objective.

**Ramanan Ramanathan**

**Former (Founder) Mission Director, Atal Innovation Mission, and Additional Secretary, NITI Aayog, Government of India**

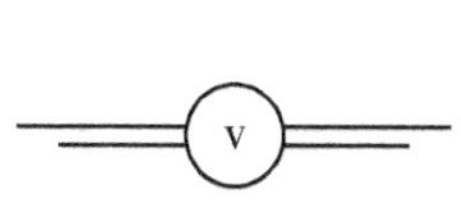

# *Why Is This Book Different?*

What sets this book apart is that it's not just another textbook filled with theory. Instead, it's a practical guide packed with real, easy-to-follow strategies that you can apply directly to transform the learning experience in your school. It recognizes the challenges schools face in bringing STEM education to life and offers actionable solutions that are simple, effective, and impactful.

Whether you're a teacher, a school leader, or even a parent, this book speaks to you in a relatable and accessible way. It's filled with tips and ideas to help you go beyond merely teaching facts—to truly inspire students to think, explore, and grow. This isn't just a book to read; it's a resource to help you spark meaningful change and make a lasting impact on how children learn and approach the world around them.

As Albert Einstein famously said, *"Education is not the learning of facts, but the training of the mind to think."* That's exactly the mission of this book: to inspire young minds to think critically and creatively, equipping them to embrace a future full of possibilities with confidence and curiosity.

So, let's not wait any longer. Together, let's embark on this exciting journey to reimagine education and make a difference by takingone step at a time...

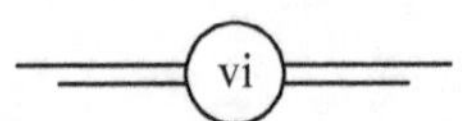

# Chapter 1

# An Idea that Changed Everything

Our experiences shape our beliefs, and these conscious moments make us who we are. Truly, the best teacher in life is experience itself. Whatever we want to learn deeply and absorb quickly, we must experience it.

From my own journey, I've discovered that hands-on, activity-based learning not only helps us understand concepts but also allows us to retain that knowledge longer. I'm sure we can all agree with the timeless wisdom of the renowned philosopher Confucius, who expressed in the 6th century BC:

*'I hear and I forget, I see and I remember, I do and I understand.'*

When I first experienced this principle firsthand, it completely transformed my perspective. Let me share how it all began.

You might remember the famous tagline, *"An idea can change your life."* For me, the idea of creating an "activity-based learning" approach not only changed my life—from being an engineer to becoming an educator—but also revolutionized the learning experiences of countless students.

## *A Passion for Transformation*

Hello, my name is Chetanya Sahu. My passion for innovation, combined with my engineering background, has fueled my journey from a curious student to an entrepreneur dedicated to transforming education. My zeal for doing something new,

learning through observation, and embracing challenges has driven me to create solutions that prepare schools and students for the future.

This book is a culmination of my decade-long experience working with hundreds of schools to make them future-ready. It aligns with the principles of NEP 2020, NCF 2023, and CBSE's current requirements to foster innovation among students. My goal is to provide you with actionable insights to implement Activity-Based-Learning (ABL) effectively.

This may be your #1 guide for the transformation you are looking for in your school. You'll find practical strategies, case studies, and a proven 10-step ABL framework to transform your students into confident problem-solvers. This will save you time & money by not using a hit & trial method for the desired success from STEM. I am 100% confident that with this 10-step ABL framework you will create your own #1 story of success by transforming your students into problem-solvers.

But first, let me share the journey that led me here.

## *From Engineer to Educator*

After completing my engineering degree, while most of my peers pursued jobs or higher studies, I was driven by a desire to make learning more engaging and meaningful. I found immense joy in hands-on experiences like practical labs and workshops, which significantly enhanced my understanding of complex subjects.

From 2009 to 2013, my team and I developed robotics kits, sensor modules, and development boards for undergraduate students. We conducted over 500 Robotics & Embedded Systems programs at premier institutions across India and Bangladesh, including IITs, NITs, and BUET Dhaka.

During this journey, I noticed a troubling trend: over 80% of engineering students were unclear about why they were pursuing the field. Many were driven by parental aspirations, peer pressure, or societal expectations, rather than genuine interest. This misalignment was a root cause of the industry's concern: *"Employment is not the problem; employability is."*

This realization left me baffled. I began questioning my own purpose and felt an inner calling to address the root cause of this problem. The solution, I realized, lay in igniting curiosity and fostering skills in younger students. By creating strong foundations through experiential learning, I could help them make informed career choices.

## *The Turning Point*

This introspection led me to make a bold decision: I shut down my company to focus entirely on working with young minds. I began extensive research to find ways to make learning fun, effective, and meaningful for children.

With support from the Department of Science & Technology (DST), Government of India, and a grant from MSME, I developed a product called **MechanzO**—a DIY robotics kit designed for children aged 6-16 years. These kits unleashed creativity in young learners, allowing them to build robots, program them, and develop critical thinking skills. Launched at IIT Bombay, this single product has impacted over 2,00,000 children, sparking their passion for STEM. *Children just love it!*

## Why This Book?

Today, the world is rapidly embracing STEM education to prepare for advancements in technology and science. Yet, many schools struggle to implement STEM effectively, often wasting valuable time and resources.

This book is designed to guide progressive schools toward becoming future-ready by successfully integrating STEM education. It offers a clear roadmap to nurture the future skills students need while avoiding common pitfalls.

I am 100% confident that if you follow the 10-step ABL framework shared in this book, you'll create your own success story, transforming your students into innovative problem-solvers. Let's begin this exciting journey together!

A few ***Accolades in the journey of transforming Education:***

"Honored to be appreciated by former President of India and renowned scientist **Dr. APJ Abdul Kalam** for driving innovation in education."

"Honored to share the impact of the STEM program with the Former Vice President of India, **Shri M. Venkaiah Naidu.**"

"Thrilled to be featured among the top startup entrepreneurs on **ET Now's *Lufthansa Runway to Success* TV** show."

**"Invited by Prof. S. K. Kak, Vice Chancellor (now Former) of UP Technical University,** to train their faculties in Embedded **System."**

# Chapter 2

# A New Chapter Begins

It was a cold December morning in Delhi. Dense fog covered the city even at 11 AM, and I sat at home, sipping coffee, lost in thoughts about my students. Being on maternity leave for a month—the longest break I'd ever taken from work as the Head of the Science Department at Veda International School—I deeply missed teaching. My passion for teaching has always been the driving force in my life.

Suddenly, a sharp pain gripped my abdomen. Alarmed, I called out to my husband, Rishi, who was fortunately at home due to the Christmas holidays. He immediately called the doctor, who advised us to visit the hospital. Unable to walk comfortably, Rishi sought help from our neighbours, Abhimanyu and Meera. They arrived in minutes and helped us get to the car. Before leaving, I requested Meera to look after my son, Rajat, who was in Grade 4 at Veda International School. I knew he would be comfortable spending time with Akshat, Meera's son and Rajat's close friend. Rajat & Akshat are childhood buddies. Akshat is an intelligent, multi-talent child, good at studies, creative, and an explorer.

At the hospital, the doctor admitted me due to some pregnancy related complications. On December 25th, Riya, my daughter, was born. It was a moment of immense joy, though she had to stay in an incubator for observation. The COVID restrictions meant family members couldn't visit, but video calls helped us share our happiness. A week later, on January 1st, Riya and I returned home to a warm welcome organized by Rajat and Akshat. Rajat greeted us with a trumpet he had made from a recycled bottle—simple yet thoughtful.

Shanti, our ever-dependable house help, was instrumental in helping me adjust to my new routine with baby Riya. During one of our moments at home, I noticed a homemade trumpet Rajat had crafted from scraps. It was simple yet creative, and it brought me so much joy to see this inventive side of him.

Rajat's curiosity seemed to grow day by day. One afternoon, as he was fiddling with my work chair, he asked, "Mamma, do you know how this chair moves up and down?" I played along, saying no, and his response was, "Because of the hydraulic mechanism, and the same mechanism is used in cranes." His explanation left me amazed; I couldn't recall ever discussing hydraulics with him.

The next day, Rajat was diligently completing his homework, which involved drawing different shapes. As he worked on a circle, he looked up and asked, "Why are manholes on roads round-shaped?" I gave him the best scientific answer I could, but I was genuinely impressed by his ability to question everyday things with such depth.

One particular afternoon, while I was trying to put Riya to sleep, Rajat experienced a power outage in his room. He came to me, saying, "Mamma, there's no power in my room." Assuming it was a general power failure, I reassured him. But Rajat, the investigator, checked the drawing room and noted the power was on there. He even switched on the fan in his room and found it functioning. Then he said something that left me speechless:

"Mumma, I think either there's a problem with the bulb, or the wire to the bulb is shorted somewhere."

At that moment, I realized that Rajat wasn't just asking questions—he was starting to think critically, approaching problems like an explorer determined to find answers. This shift in his mindset made me proud and reassured me that his growing curiosity and problem-solving skills were paving the way for something truly special.

# Case Study
## Transforming Education at
## Blooming Dale School

*The next day, I decided to call my mentor, Mr. Ishan Mediratta, Director of Blooming Dale School, the institution where I completed my schooling. He has been a guiding force in my teaching career, a visionary educator whose insights I've always valued. Our conversation revolved around the state of education at the school and how it was adapting to the competitive landscape.*

*Mr. Mediratta shared that despite 4–5 prominent brand-name schools opening in Baduan, Blooming Dale continued to operate at full capacity with over 4,000 students. However, they faced a churn, with approximately 200 new admissions each year offset by a similar number of dropouts. To address this, he conducted a comprehensive survey with parents and students to identify why they chose Blooming Dale. Most respondents appreciated the school's long-standing presence and convenient location in the city's heart.*

*Determined to innovate, Mr. Mediratta sought advice from his former Principal, now leading a prestigious residential school in Nainital. The Principal recommended integrating a STEM program to enhance experiential learning. While this seemed promising, Ishan Sir felt that finding the right STEM partner in Baduan would take time.*

*In the interim, he initiated a practice of monthly outdoor visits for students to places like fire stations, hospitals, markets, old age homes, fairs, government offices, and community service centers. These visits aimed to provide hands-on learning experiences and foster social awareness. The sight of students engaging in these activities in their school uniforms also helped reshape public perceptions. Blooming Dale was no longer viewed as a rote-learning institution; instead, it was gaining respect as a forward-thinking school offering holistic education.*

*Within three months, the school partnered with a Noida-based company to implement a STEM program. This partner came highly recommended by Ishan Sir's former Principal, further affirming the decision. The results were almost immediate. The school observed an increase in student retention and welcomed 30 new mid-year admissions. Based on the positive feedback, they anticipated over 150 additional admissions in the upcoming academic year.*

*This shift was not just about numbers; it marked a cultural transformation. Parents and students now viewed Blooming Dale as a progressive institution that prepared learners for the real world, equipped with critical thinking and problem-solving skills through experiential and STEM-based education.*

***Key Takeaway:*** *The case of Blooming Dale School highlights the power of innovation and adaptation in education. By embracing experiential learning and STEM, the school spin challenges into opportunities, ensuring its continued growth and relevance in a competitive environment.*

## Rajat's Creative Journey

Rajat has been surprising me lately with his innovative and creative streak. One of the most touching moments was when I noticed him crafting toys for his little sister, Riya, using scraps and parts from old toys. His ingenuity in repurposing materials left me in awe and filled me with pride.

One day, as I was working, I noticed that his room door was closed. Curious, I opened it and found him engrossed on my laptop. Thinking he was playing games, I raised my voice, and asked, "With whose permission are you playing games?" To my amazement, Rajat calmly explained that he wasn't playing games but designing on a game which he could later play it with Riya.

When I looked closer, I saw him working on animations in **Scratch**, a programming platform for kids. Overwhelmed and intrigued, I exclaimed, **"ये चल क्या रहा है!"**

I couldn't help but ask him, "Is this taught in school?" Rajat shared that he learned it from Akshat, his childhood friend, during a stayover. Akshat often made games and animations, which Rajat had eagerly picked up.

Reflecting on this, I realized how children are quick to learn from their peers. Akshat, whom I have known since he was little, has always been an exceptionally bright child. He studies at Sparsh Global School, known for its progressive educational practices.

Initially, I thought Rajat's sudden interest in creating games and animations was simply due to Akshat's influence. But regardless of this source, I was delighted to see this incredible transformation in Rajat's outlook as he embraced on a journey of creativity, exploration, designing, and by thinking critically. Moments like these remind me how important exposure and the right environment are in nurturing young minds.

## *Evening at Meera's House: A New Perspective*

That evening, I visited Meera's house to thank her for taking care of Rajat during my busy days. As we chatted, I shared the delightful incidents and observations about Rajat's growing curiosity. I mentioned how his endless "why" questions now kept me on my toes, challenging me to provide answers that satisfy his eagerness to learn.

Meera smiled knowingly and said she'd been experiencing the same with Akshat for the past year. She explained how Akshat's creativity, observational skills, and logical thinking had become his second nature. We both felt proud of these subtle yet magical transformations in our children.

Curious, I asked her, *"What do you think has triggered this shift in Akshat?"*

Meera revealed that Akshat's school, Sparsh Global School, had introduced an **Innovation STEM Program** throughout all grades of students about a year ago. She described how the program integrates science, technology, engineering, and mathematics to provide hands-on, experiential learning and it's mandatory for all the students. Through activities like coding, robotics, design thinking, and artificial intelligence, Akshat had started seeing the real-world application of concepts.

She shared how the school emphasized learning in a way that was fun yet meaningful. Akshat often hurried through his homework to make time for these activities and never missed his Tuesday STEM classes, which had become his favorite. His enthusiasm was evident when he showcased his projects, and Meera beamed with pride as she shared that he'd recently won an award in an Innovation Challenge.

Listening to Meera, I felt a mix of excitement and introspection. As a science teacher, I wondered why I hadn't explored integrated learning approaches like these before. Meera's insights opened my eyes to the potential of STEM education—not just as a subject but as a transformative way to nurture creativity, critical thinking, and problem-solving skills in children.

She also handed me a few STEM activity ideas to try with Rajat, which I eagerly accepted.

That evening, I felt a renewed sense of purpose, both as a parent and as a teacher. As a mother, I was excited to guide Rajat in exploring new skills that could shape his future. As an educator, I realized the importance of staying updated with innovative teaching methods to prepare our children for a rapidly evolving AI-driven world.

This conversation not only deepened my understanding of STEM but also inspired me to take steps toward making learning more engaging and impactful for my students and my own child.

## *My Journey into STEM: From Curiosity to Understanding*

Returning home, my curiosity about STEM education was piqued. I eagerly began exploring online resources and was amazed by the variety of STEM-based kits available. However, the abundance of options left me wondering which would be best suited for Rajat.

After thoroughly analyzing reviews, I decided to order three kits. When the kits arrived, Rajat's excitement was contagious. He dove right into the **"MechanzO" kit**, which became his favorite because of its metal parts, gears, and endless possibilities for innovation. Within days, he started building mechanical shapes and robots, and in just a month, he was not only creating stable models but also programming them. Every time he completed a new project, his sense of accomplishment was evident, and he eagerly shared his creations with friends and family.

However, as weeks passed, Rajat reached a plateau. He seemed unsure of what to explore next, and I realized that while the kit provided hands-on learning, it lacked structured guidance to deepen his understanding. This prompted me to question: *Is STEM only about robotics?*

Determined to uncover the broader scope of STEM and its long-term benefits, I delved into more research. My findings were enlightening and gave me a clearer picture of how STEM goes beyond robotics.

## *What I Learned About STEM*

1. **STEM Is a Holistic Approach to Learning:** STEM integrates Science, Technology, Engineering, and Mathematics, but its essence lies in teaching students to think critically, solve problems creatively, and work collaboratively. It's about applying theoretical knowledge gained in classroom to real-world challenges.

2. **Beyond Robotics:** While robotics is a prominent aspect of STEM, it's just one part of a larger framework. STEM also includes:

   - **Coding and Programming:** Understanding the language of computers.

   - **Design Thinking:** Creating solutions through brainstorming and prototyping.

   - **Mathematical Modeling:** Applying math to solve practical problems.

   - **Engineering Principles:** Exploring how structures and systems work.

3. **Hands-On Learning:** STEM emphasizes experiential learning, making abstract concepts tangible. Activities like building models, conducting experiments, or programming games make learning engaging and effective.

4. **Future-Ready Skills:** STEM nurtures 21st-century skills such as adaptability, teamwork, creativity, and digital literacy. These are essential for thriving in an AI-driven and technology-focused world.

5. **Lifelong Benefits:** STEM doesn't just prepare children for careers in science or engineering; it equips them with a mindset that values exploration, innovation, and resilience—qualities that are valuable in any field.

## *What's Next for Rajat*

With this newfound understanding, I realized that Rajat's journey with STEM needed to go beyond kits. He required structured exposure to concepts, challenges, and mentorship to continue growing his skills.

This realization has inspired me to advocate for better STEM learning resources in schools and at home. For progressive educators, parents, and schools, understanding STEM's potential is crucial in shaping a generation that not only adapts to but leads the technological advancements of tomorrow.

I'm excited to continue exploring this journey, both as a teacher and as a parent, to help Rajat and others discover the magic of STEM.

I am sure that my research as a teacher will be useful for all Progressive Schools, Educators, and Parents. My research summary will surely help understand STEM and its benefits. I have summarised it in a way that any novice can also understand STEM.

# CHAPTER 3

# Shaping Minds with STEM

**Let us first understand what STEM Education is?** STEM education is a teaching and learning approach that is a unique combination of **Science, Technology, Engineering, and Mathematics.** To be precise, STEM education primarily focuses on hands-on and problem-based learning methodologies.

After understanding STEM Education, let's understand **why it is getting so important?** With **STEM**, it is not the teaching of one subject but it is the amalgamation of all four subjects as a comprehensive one taught through an interdisciplinary curriculum. This helps students deal with real-world situations and apply their learning to create, innovate, and discover new things.

STEM **emphasizes on developing logical and critical thinking skills by allowing students to learn and understand concepts from the perspective of the real world**. STEM education equips students with the skills required to succeed in their respective careers, whether it is in a job or in entrepreneurship.

**The Benefits of STEM Education:**

1.  Improves Creativity

2.  In the current AI world, it helps schools to position themselves as future ready

3.  Increases Team Collaboration

4.  Empowers Critical Thinking Skills

5.  Boosts Curiosity

6.  Improves Cognitive Skills

7.  Introduces STEM Careers at Early Stages

8.  Teaches You to Take an Initiative

9.  Boosts Socio-Emotional Learning

10. Develops Communication Skills

11. Develops Scientific Temperament

**As every coin has two sides, let us understand both the Pros and Cons of STEM Education:**

## *Pros of STEM Education:*

➤ *Allows to understand the practical application of concepts.*

➤ *Develops communication, critical thinking, cognitive skills, etc.*

➤ *Enhances retention of learning for a longer time or even permanently.*

➤ *Helps in preparing students for the future workforce.*

## *Cons of STEM Education:*

➤ **Lacks** *proper guidelines/set of protocols.*

➤ *Implementing STEM might get costly if it is experimented with hit & trial.*

➤ *Requires a significant amount of time, as the learning is integrated into behaviour over a period.*

## *A Journey of Transformation: STEM and Rajat's Remarkable Growth*

After gaining a thorough understanding of STEM, I was determined to find the right guidance for Rajat to fully embrace and adapt to this new integrated way of learning to prepare him for the future. My search for experienced, outcome-driven STEM educators in the Delhi-NCR area led me to a Noida-based organization with over a decade of experience in STEM education.

During my visit to their office, I was impressed by their comprehensive curriculum and hands-on activities. To my surprise, they were the same organization behind the highly-praised STEM program at Sparsh Global School! This serendipity boosted my confidence in their approach. After meeting their mentors, I enrolled Rajat in their yearlong STEM program, which involved weekly Monday evening classes.

## *Rajat's STEM Journey: From Rote to Growth*

As Rajat progressed through the program, the changes were transformative:

1. **Visible Learning Outcomes:**

   - He explored Robotics, Coding, and Electronics, mastering skills that were previously unfamiliar to him.

   - His creative and technical abilities flourished, evident in his class projects and competitions.

2. **Mindset Evolution:**

   - Rajat developed **critical thinking and problem-solving skills**, qualities essential in today's world.

- He became more curious and confident, embracing exploration and understanding concepts deeply before advancing.

3. **Academic Revival:**

- In earlier grades, traditional learning methods had dimmed his interest in studies.

- Post-STEM, he became an eager learner, and his academic performance improved significantly. His teachers now praised his initiative and creativity in class.

4. **Confidence Boost:**

- Once hesitant and shy, Rajat now boldly shared his ideas and participated actively in projects. His innovative mindset earned him **first prize on Science Day** for his unique project.

## *Beyond Individual Impact*

As a teacher and mother, witnessing Rajat's transformation has been overwhelming by inspiring. His journey is a testament to the power of STEM education in fostering a growth mindset and has helped to unlock his inner hidden potential.

This experience motivated me to think beyond Rajat. I realized that such a transformative program shouldn't be limited to just one child. It was time to share this with others, particularly my school Principal, so that more students could benefit from this program.

## *STEM: A Case Study in Transformation*

Rajat's journey is a compelling real-world example of how STEM can reshape a child's approach to learning and life. It has helped him transition from being a passive learner to an active problem-solver, instilling confidence, curiosity, and resilience in him.

With this case study in hand, I'm eager to advocate for STEM adoption in schools, ensuring more children to experience its far-reaching benefits. Together, we can nurture a generation of thinkers, creators, and innovators ready to thrive in the future

## Research Summary: Introducing STEM Education in Schools

As I prepared to present the idea of implementing a STEM program in our school to the Principal, I delved deeply into its benefits and practical implementation. Below is a summarized version of my findings:

## Why STEM Education is Crucial During School Years

1.  **Early Brain Development:**

    - Childhood is the most crucial phase for cognitive development, and introducing STEM during these formative years can shape a child's problem-solving and critical-thinking abilities.

2.  **Real-World Connections:**

    - STEM bridges classroom concepts with real-world applications, keeping students engaged and curious about their surroundings.

3.  **Fostering Interest and Motivation:**

    - Experiential STEM activities motivate children to explore and persevere in completing tasks, fostering a sense of accomplishment.

## 4. Career Readiness:

- Early exposure to STEM fields prepares students for future career opportunities in technology-driven industries, ensuring they remain competitive in a rapidly evolving world.

## *Benefits of Incorporating STEM in Schools*

### 1. Enhances Creativity and Innovation:

- Encourages students to think out of the box and design creative solutions to real-world challenges.

### 2. Develops Critical and Analytical Thinking:

- Helps students break down problems systematically and develop logical solutions.

### 3. Encourages Collaboration and Teamwork:

- STEM projects often involve group activities, teaching students the value of collaboration and communication.

### 4. Increases Engagement in Learning:

- Practical, hands-on learning keeps students excited and more connected to the subject matter.

### 5. Aligns with Future Needs:

- Prepares students to excel in fields like AI, robotics, coding, and engineering, which are in high demand globally.

## *Key Steps to Implement a STEM Program in School*

### 1. Choosing the Right STEM Partner:

- Partner with an experienced STEM education provider with a proven curriculum and hands-on activities.

2. **Training Teachers:**

- Offer professional development sessions for teachers to equip them with skills to facilitate STEM learning effectively.

3. **Starting with Basics:**

- Introduce foundational STEM activities for younger grades and progressively expand the scope for older students.

4. **Infrastructure and Resources:**

- Allocate space and resources for STEM labs equipped with tools like robotics kits, coding software, and 3D printers.

5. **Integration into Curriculum:**

- Seamlessly incorporate STEM into existing subjects like science, math, and technology rather than treating it as an add-on.

6. **Parent and Student Orientation:**

- Organize workshops to help parents and students understand the long-term benefits of STEM education.

7. **Monitoring and Evaluation:**

- Regularly assess the program's impact on student learning outcomes and interest in STEM fields.

## *Expected Outcomes for Our School*

1. **Enhanced Student Engagement and Performance:**

- Students will become active learners, improving both academic and personal growth.

2. **Elevated School Reputation:**

- Adopting an advanced STEM program can set our school apart as a pioneer in holistic, future-ready education.

3. **Empowered Teachers:**

- STEM training will enrich teachers' instructional methods, making them facilitators of innovative learning.

4. **Future-Ready Students:**

- Equipping them with essential 21st-century skills, thus helping students to have an edge in their future careers and life.

This comprehensive research highlights the transformative power of STEM education and makes a compelling case for its integration into our school. By investing in STEM, we invest in the future of our students, equipping them with skills to thrive in a tech-driven world which is the need of the hour.

With this proposal, I hope to inspire our pPrincipal to take the first step toward a brighter future for thousands of students.

# CHAPTER 4

# STEM in Action

STEM is important in Early Childhood Education because schools play a vital role in imparting knowledge to students. After all, a person spends nearly 1/5th of their life going to school. STEM education focuses on building habits that will help children throughout their lives, from critical thinking, problem-solving, and creative thinking to computation and interpersonal skills. They learn how to apply all of these skills to their daily lives in order to build a better world around them.

To understand the learning objectives of STEM at different educational stages, here's an overview of how it is integrated at each level:

1. **Elementary School:** One might think that students under five years of age can do little when it comes to STEM. However, researchers have found that children in this age group are exceptionally quick at learning and exhibiting great creativity and technical abilities.

## A Foundation of Curiosity and Joy

The foundational experiences for K-2 students in STEM focus on sparking curiosity, encouraging exploration, and building a positive, hands-on relationship with learning.

By introducing them to foundational concepts in science, math, engineering, and technology through playful, inquiry-based activities, students will develop an early love for STEM and the skills necessary to navigate the world. At this stage, the goal is to foster curiosity, creativity, and a sense of wonder, allowing them to see the world as a place full of interesting questions to explore and answers to discover.

Focus on **Problem-Solving and Communication Skills** for grades 3-5.New ideas include:

➢ Solving problems using **Design Thinking**.

➢ Exploring **Cause and Effect** through **collaborative activities**.

➢ Conducting **hands-on experiments** to enhance understanding.

➢ Investigating concepts like **Forces and Motion**.

➢ Applying **Math in real-life scenarios**.

➢ Engaging in **Technological Exploration** and improving **Digital Literacy**.

➢ Encourage **Creativity and Teamwork** through:

- Building and constructing projects.
- Presenting ideas to peers or groups.
- Collaborative **group work**.
- Writing, reporting, and storytelling.

➢ Integrate **Art and Engineering** with:

- Activities combining creativity and engineering concepts.
- Exploring the role of **technology in daily life**.

➤ Promote **Sustainability and Inquiry-Based Learning** by:

- Understanding and practicing **sustainable habits**.

- Encouraging **question-driven exploration**.

STEM education should empower students to explore new ideas, deepen their understanding of scientific and mathematical principles, and develop the ability to apply their learning to solve everyday problems. The emphasis should be on fostering curiosity, building confidence, and helping students see the direct connection between what they learn in school and the world around them. By giving them opportunities to engage in hands-on projects, solve real-world challenges, and communicate their findings, we prepare them to become thoughtful, creative, and capable problem-solvers who can contribute to their communities and the world.

2. **Middle School**

**Building Independence and Deepening Understanding**

In grades 6-8, students should begin to shift toward more independent, critical thinking. This transition involves encouraging inquiry, problem-solving, self-regulation, and collaborative learning. By helping students reflect on their learning process, set goals, and develop their ability to analyze and solve problems on their own, we are preparing them for greater success in STEM and other academic areas as they move into higher education and the workforce. The emphasis should be on empowering students to take responsibility for their learning while giving them the tools to think critically, creatively, and independently.

Students should also begin to develop a deeper understanding of themselves and others. At this stage they will gain insights into their own strengths, weaknesses, and learning styles while also learn to appreciate and collaborate with diverse perspectives. By fostering self-awareness, emotional intelligence, empathy, and social understanding, students will build the foundation for becoming confident, responsible, and thoughtful individuals who can navigate academic challenges and social dynamics with resilience and empathy. These skills will serve them not only in STEM but also in all areas of their lives as they grow into young adults.

Therefore, courses are designed to make students curious to learn more. The objective here is to teach them how to learn, not what to learn. This enables them to pursue their interests early on while also being aware of the career options available after taking STEM courses.

3. **High School**

   Students are in their teens during high school, a time when they are searching for their identity and making career choices. Hence, the programs focus on the application of subjects in a challenging and rigorous manner.

## *Preparing for Advanced Learning and Real-World Applications*

By the end of grades 9-10, students should have developed a deeper understanding of complex STEM concepts and be equipped with the skills necessary to engage with these subjects critically and creatively. They should have honed their problem-solving abilities, developed strong communication and collaboration skills, and cultivated independence in their learning. At this stage, students are building a foundation for more advanced study in STEM, preparing them for success in high school and beyond. The key is to encourage them to think critically, work creatively, and approach learning with curiosity and confidence.

To encourage students to think deeply and solve problems creatively, it's essential to foster an environment that values curiosity, exploration, and risk-taking. By providing opportunities for inquiry-based learning, problem-based learning, and interdisciplinary thinking, educators can help students develop the critical thinking and creative problem-solving skills they need to navigate complex subjects. Encouraging reflection, collaboration, and the use of real-world tools and examples will empower students to approach challenges with confidence, creativity, and a deeper understanding of the world around them.

One day, I went to pick up Rajat after his STEM class and met the CEO of the company. I discussed with him to gain an expert's perspective on STEM and his experience in promoting innovation among young kids, as well as how it could be implemented in schools so that every child could benefit. The interaction was as follows:

## *Implementing STEM into the classroom curriculum*

Due to the overall low performance of students in STEM courses, there is an emerging need to address the gaps in the education system. Teachers can integrate STEM learning into the classroom curriculum by:

Acquainting students with modern **educational technology**. Giving them access to computers during classes for learning purposes broadens their minds. The internet (limited/guided) and various applications are resourceful tools for information.

1. Introducing words like "experiment", "model" and "design" in questions. This approach allows students to explore and put their skills into practice, employing creativity at its peak and ultimately preparing them for real-life challenges. For example, a teacher can ask students to design a model of a system that will curb global warming.

2. Identifying real-life problems and requiring solutions. By empowering students with issues that occur daily, they will discover that real-world problems have numerous solutions. These activities promote teamwork and effective communication, which are essential in today's world.

3. In STEM classrooms, structured activities and lessons can be developed to provide hands-on experience. Promoting active learning and practice in classrooms engage students. A teacher can also invite industry experts to inspire students by giving them a new perspective on science, math, and technology.

Mentors/Coaches who implement STEM learning in their classrooms help shape future leaders of the country. Encouraging students on the importance of these disciplines and involving them helps them illustrate their ideas. STEM learning is essential to the nation's economy and the increasing competition with other industrialized countries. Schools should advise parents on the benefits of this type of learning, as it is crucial for their child's future. The potential gap anticipated to emerge in the next decade due to technological advancement will require a substantial workforce equipped with STEM education.

Here a study is also shared that was published in the Economic Times about Why popularizing STEM-based education must be a priority.

**Read more at:** https://bit.ly/economictimes-STEM

After gathering all the research and observing Rajat's transformation, my inner self urged me, "Rohini, you must share this eye-opening perspective with your school Principal."

With this determination, I went to my school during the final exams to meet the Principal and discuss the STEM program.

## *Meeting the Principal*

I shared my findings with her, highlighting the tangible changes I had observed in Rajat—his creativity, problem-solving skills, and the confidence STEM had instilled in him. The Principal was intrigued by the idea and curious to know more about Rajat's progress. She even took time to meet Rajat personally and review some of his work.

While she found the concept fascinating, there were natural apprehensions:

1.  **Lack of Technology Background:**

    - The Principal expressed concerns about understanding and managing the program herself, as she didn't come from a technology-oriented background.

## 2. Absence of Skilled STEM Teachers:

- The school did not have experienced faculty to teach STEM subjects effectively.

Despite these concerns, her progressive and visionary mindset stood out. She recognized the potential impact such a program could have on the students and expressed her willingness to explore further.

## *Next Steps*

With her support, we prepared a plan to present this innovative program to the school management. To address the challenges of expertise and implementation, we agreed on the need to engage an external expert or organization specializing in STEM education. This step would ensure proper guidance, training, and resources, setting a strong foundation for the program's success.

This collaboration marked a significant milestone, giving me hope that Rajat's inspiring journey with STEM could pave the way for countless other students to embrace curiosity, innovation, and 21st-century skills.

## *Presenting STEM to School Management*

In January 2023, my Principal and I together presented the long-term benefits of introducing STEM education to our school management. We crafted a detailed proposal that showcased how STEM could transform not just the students but also the school's reputation as a pioneer in progressive education.

## *Key Highlights of the Presentation*

1.  **Why STEM Education Matters:**
    - We emphasized the growing importance of STEM skills in a technology-driven world and how early exposure prepares students for future careers.
    - Highlighted STEM's role in fostering critical thinking, creativity, and problem-solving—essential for 21st-century skills.

2.  **Benefits for Students:**
    - Improved engagement and understanding of real-world applications of concepts.
    - Enhanced academic performance through experiential and hands-on learning.
    - Development of a growth mindset, encouraging curiosity and innovation.

3.  **Benefits for the School:**
    - Positioning as a leader in progressive education, attracting more students and parents seeking holistic learning.
    - Strengthening teacher training, equipping educators with modern teaching techniques.
    - Creating a culture of innovation and collaboration within the school community.

4.  **Addressing Concerns:**
    - Proposed partnering with an experienced STEM organization to manage curriculum, teacher training, and implementation.
    - Highlighted the ease of integrating STEM into the existing curriculum with proper planning and support.

## *Outcome of the Presentation*

The school management appreciated the comprehensive presentation and acknowledged the potential of STEM and how the progress would to impact positively on the students' futures. While there were initial questions about cost and logistics, the long-term benefits outweighed the challenges.

With the management's support, we decided to initiate the STEM program for the upcoming academic year, starting with teacher training and resource planning. It felt like a significant step toward creating a future-ready school, and I was thrilled to see the vision take shape

## *Key Learnings for Implementing a STEM Program in Schools*

Through our discussions with various STEM education providers and an in-depth review of their deliverables, we gathered critical insights into the practical challenges and solutions for successfully implementing a STEM program. Below are the summarized learnings that guided our decision-making and served as a reference for other schools:

1. **Selecting the Right STEM Kits and Curriculum**

   - **Start Simple, Evolve Gradually:** Begin with STEM kits suitable for the students' age and skill levels, ensuring they can be scaled or replaced as students advance.

   - **Curriculum Alignment:** Choose kits and programs that integrate seamlessly with the school curriculum while promoting hands-on learning.

- **Customizable Content:** Opt for kits that allow flexibility to create projects relevant to real-world applications, sparking curiosity and innovation.

2. **The Role of Experts and Mentors**

   - **Engaging STEM Experts:** Partner with experienced organizations to design and implement a structured program tailored to the school's needs.

   - **Teacher Involvement:** Train existing teachers to act as facilitators, supported by an external mentor or a team of specialists. This reduces dependency on a single expert.

   - **Dedicated STEM Mentor:** Consider hiring a full-time mentor with a STEM background who can ensure consistent program delivery across grades.

3. **Balancing Mandatory vs. Optional Participation**

   - **Make It Inclusive:** Initially, introduce STEM as a mandatory part of the curriculum to encourage participation and showcase its benefits.

   - **Flexibility for Advanced Students:** Offer optional advanced modules for interested students as the program matures.

4. **Managing Costs**

   - **Transparent Budgeting:** Decide upfront whether to absorb the cost in the development budget or pass it on to parents after demonstrating outcomes.

   - **Phased Investment:** Start small but be impactful, focusing on quality over quantity to minimize initial costs. Expand as the program gains traction.

- **Long-Term Partnerships:** Partner with organizations that provide affordable subscription models or shared resources, reducing financial strain.

5. **Timetable Integration**

   - **Reworking Schedules:** Allocate two consecutive periods weekly for STEM classes. Collaboration between teachers and administrators can help accommodate this change.
   - **Practice Time:** Create STEM labs or clubs where students can practice and work on projects outside class hours.

6. **Assessing Student Learning**

   - **Project-Based Assessments:** Evaluate students based on their projects, teamwork, creativity, and ability to solve real-world problems.
   - **Progress Reports:** Maintain portfolios for each student to track their progress over time.
   - **Regular Showcases:** Organize STEM fairs and competitions to let students present their projects, engaging parents and the community.

7. **Selecting the Right Partner**

   - **Comprehensive Deliverables:** Look for providers who offer end-to-end solutions, including curriculum design, teacher training, resources, and ongoing support.
   - **Customizability:** Choose a partner who understands the school's unique requirements and can adapt their offerings accordingly.
   - **Sustainability:** Ensure the program is scalable and self-sustaining in the long run, reducing dependency on external support.

By addressing these concerns systematically, we gained the confidence to move forward with STEM implementation. With the expert we chose, we ensured that the program was not only educationally enriching but also operationally feasible and sustainable for the school.

This exercise reaffirmed that while STEM implementation has challenges, a well-planned approach can overcome them, unlocking immense potential for students and the school.

# Chapter 5

# The 10-Step ABL (Activity-Based Learning) Framework

Let's discuss the makers of this **10-Step ABL (Activity-based Learning) framework** later, first let's understand how this framework guarantees success. **This framework would resolve** most of your possible objections related to implementation and at the same time give a clear direction for right execution. The simplicity of this framework makes it easy to implement and gives confidence of success. This framework has been developed after analysing the failure of hundreds of Schools in not getting the desired outcome after implementing STEM Education.

1. **Set Clear Goals**

   - Develop a **3-5-year vision** for the STEM program with well-defined yearly and quarterly milestones.

   - Clearly document these goals to avoid confusion and ensure alignment across all stakeholders, creating measurable checkpoints for progress

   - Conduct **periodic reviews** to track progress and make course corrections as needed.

2. **Progressive Curriculum, Content & Assessment**

   - Create an **age-appropriate, grade-wise curriculum** aligned with NCF (National Curriculum Framework) and NEP (National Education Policy) guidelines.

- Activities should focus on developing both core and future-ready skills (e.g., critical thinking, collaboration).

- Use a variety of resources: **videos, stories, presentations, quizzes**, etc., to match diverse learning needs.

- Assessment should be **project-based** and tied to skill development, with results integrated into students' progress reports.

3. **Select the Right Hardware & Software**

   - Hardware and software are chosen to match the curriculum's goals, ensuring adaptability, ensuring they can adapt as students' progress. Examples include:
     - **Robotics** kits
     - **AI and Machine Learning** platforms
     - **3D design and coding** tools
     - **IoT and simulation** software

   - Avoid managing hardware internally—partner with **hardware experts** to prevent innovation bottlenecks.

4. **Trained Mentors Are the Key**

   - Invest in **expert mentors** with experience in STEM education. A skilled team ensures better implementation than relying solely on a single STEM teacher.

   - Establish a **review system** led by a program director to track classroom activities and outcomes.

5. **Learn Beyond the Classroom**

   - Implement a **Learning Management System (LMS)** for anytime, anywhere learning.

- Provide students with access to class content, practice quizzes, and assessments through the LMS.

- Enable Principals and teachers to monitor students' progress digitally.

## 6. Parents as Key Stakeholders

- Orient parents about the purpose and benefits of STEM education through workshops and PTMs (Parent-Teacher Meetings).

- Showcase students' projects during PTMs and allow parents to track progress via the LMS.

- Include **take-home activities** to engage parents in their child's learning journey.

## 7. Industry Exposure

- Invite industry experts, researchers, and alumni working in STEM fields to interact with students, especially those in Grade 6 and above.

- Organize **field visits** to STEM-related industries to help students connect classroom learning with real-world applications.

## 8. Competitive Spirit

- Host **inter-school STEM competitions and exhibitions** to foster peer learning and encourage creativity.

- Prepare students for participation in national and international STEM challenges to boost their confidence and exposure.

9. **Advocacy and Accountability**

   - Have a dedicated **Program Director** to oversee the STEM program's implementation and track progress regularly.

   - Regular review of classroom outcomes and adjust the curriculum or goals as needed for continuous improvement.

10. **Create a Creativity Space**

    - Design an inviting **innovation lab** or space that inspires creativity and critical thinking.

    - Ensure the environment encourages students to experiment, ideate, and innovate freely.

## *Why Schools Fail Without This Framework*

Many schools struggle with STEM implementation due to:

➢ **Unclear objectives** leading to inconsistent execution.

➢ **Lack of trained mentors** resulting in poor delivery.

➢ **Improper integration** of curriculum, hardware, and software.

➢ **Minimal parental involvement** causing a disconnect in student progress.

The 10-Step ABL Framework systematically addresses these challenges, ensuring clarity, alignment, and scalability.

## *Time and Effort Optimization*

This framework eliminates trial-and-error approaches by providing a proven roadmap. Its simplicity enables:

➢ Faster implementation.

➢ Reduced resource wastage.

➢ Better engagement from students, teachers, and parents.

By leveraging the **ABL Framework**, schools can achieve transformative outcomes in STEM education with confidence, ensuring long-term success for their students.

The makers of the **10-Step ABL Framework** concluded by reiterating the essence and its simplicity. While it may seem straightforward, it was meticulously crafted based on insights gained from working with **400+ schools**, pinpointing exactly where schools often fall short in achieving meaningful outcomes in STEM education.

## *Key Takeaway: Long-Term Thinking*

The expert emphasized that schools must approach STEM with a **progressive, long-term vision** rather than treating it as a short-term initiative or merely an investment in hardware kits. This perspective shift ensures sustained impact and prevents schools from missing the true potential of STEM programs.

## *The Testimonial That Sealed the Deal*

The highlight of the session was the testimonial from the Principal of **Sparsh Global School**, which reinforced the value of the ABL framework and the STEM program:

> "From a learning aspect, we have been able to enhance our children's learning retention by 60% through STEM education. Our children are transforming, becoming better, more creative, more exploratory, and more skilled day by day with this impactful program. 'Awesome!' is the word for the STEM Program. And the way it is implemented in our school, 'Commendable!' is the word for the team who is on their toes to support us. Highly supportive and reachable."

> "I have no doubt in saying that the STEM Program is successfully implemented in our school because of the ABL Education team."

## Swift Decision by the School Management

With the support of our visionary school management, who appreciated the value of this transformative framework, the decision to **launch the program in the new academic year** was made in just **10 days**.

## A Personal Milestone

For me, this journey not only brought transformative learning to our school but also marked a personal achievement: I was entrusted with the additional responsibility of **STEM Teacher Coordinator** alongside my role as **HoD-Science**.

This is just the beginning of a transformative journey for our students, and I am thrilled to be part of it.

# CHAPTER 6

# Defining the Vision of STEM Education

Now that you have understood the concept of STEM education, let me help you understand the major goals & objectives of STEM. The major goals & objectives of STEM education are:

## Goal #1: Utilization of Information & Insights

STEM aims to enable students to utilize information & insights in the scientific field, technological area, engineering & mathematics. The concept allows students to explore a wide range of content & projects.

## Goal #2: Implementation of Best Practices

Students must be able to implement the best practices in all the disciplines of STEM. The long-term aim is to develop a stronger aptitude for these four disciplines.

## Goal #3: Knowledge Acquisition & Creativity

Students should acquire knowledge in the four STEM areas and become capable of innovating new ideas.

To sum up the three major goals, I would like to quote an example here.

**Example:** The teacher may ask students to prepare an **"Eco-friendly Cooling Machine"** in the lab. Here, the students may approach the teachers for references. Additionally, they may visit a carpenter or potter to understand the process that goes around creating the tool, such as –

➢ Learning about various materials

➢ Choosing the right material

➢ Working on the project

➢ Filing, angle cutting, or using the right clay

➢ Finishing the job

This way, students get an opportunity to explore their options by –

## *RESEARCHING + THINKING + APPLYING = CREATING*

## *Components of STEM Education*

➢ **Problem-Based Learning**

In this type of learning, students collect data, analyze it, come up with scientific explanations, and identify the problems to conduct research activities. Further, they develop a prototype to solve the problem and then come up with the best solution for it. This way, students apply mathematics and technology to real-life problems.

➢ **Rigorous Learning**

Rigorous learning is a way of learning that is applied to the lessons in such a way that it encourages the students to question their assumptions and think deeply. It keeps them away from learning for memorization and recall of information during the exams.

➢ **Career, Technology, and Life Skills:** This involves making students skilled in the subjects they are learning. It puts major emphasis on student learning through projects, internships, and hands-on experiences. It aims to build critical thinking, collaboration, communication, and creativity among the students.

➢ **Personalization of Learning:** Personalized learning involves a shift in the methods of instruction from teacher-led classrooms to more student-centred learning. In this approach, the student has the choice to learn at their own pace, choose their project of interest, and get assessed accordingly.

➢ **School Community and Belonging:** This type of learning involves students gaining knowledge about giving respect, accepting individuals as they are, and inclusion. It aims to allow students to share their feelings and experiences with other students and gain perspectives.

➢ **Connection To the Broader and External Community:** This involves making the students ambitious and outward-looking. The students are given local environment and community organizations as learning resources. They understand issues in their surroundings and work toward solving them.

STEM Education is a part of education for more than two decades globally, but why is it necessary for the Indian Education Sector?

➢ It enables better inquisitive mindsets among students.

➢ It encourages critical thinking among them.

➢ It helps them to think logically.

➢ It prepares students to be better leaders and decision-makers in the future.

Students are taught skills and professionalism in the early stages of education.

# Time to Make the Right Choice

With all that you have learnt about STEM education and its immense potential, the choice is yours to empower your child or students with skills that will prepare them for the future. In today's fast-paced, technology-driven world, **equipping children with STEM skills is no longer optional—it's essential**!

## *Why You Need the Right Partner*

STEM education isn't just a short-term program; it's a **transformational journey**. Selecting the right partner for implementation is critical because:

1. **Expertise Matters**:

   - A good partner ensures that STEM programs are aligned with long-term learning goals, not just surface-level outcomes.

   - They guide you through curriculum planning, hardware/ software selection, training, and assessments.

2. **Avoid Costly Mistakes**:

   - Many schools dive into STEM without a proper strategy, leading to **wasted time and resources**.

   - A clear and structured implementation approach avoids pitfalls and maximizes results.

3. **Stakeholder Engagement**:

- The right partner involves all stakeholders—students, parents, teachers, and management—ensuring a smooth adoption and sustained interest in the program.

## *Recommendation*

If you are considering STEM education for your school or children, I highly recommend consulting **Mr. Chetanya Sahu,** a seasoned entrepreneur & an expert in STEM Education. Having worked with him at my school, I can vouch for his ability to guide you to tailored STEM programs for your children that deliver measurable outcomes and long-term benefits.

## *Contact Details:*

**WhatsApp: +91-9211786062**

## *Final Note*

Adopting STEM education is more than just staying updated with trends—it's about preparing students for the challenges of tomorrow. Whether you are a parent, teacher, or school administrator, the decisions you make today will shape the innovators and leaders of tomorrow.

Remember, **it's not just about investing in kits or technology; it's about building a culture of innovation and curiosity**. Make the right choice, and watch the transformation unfold.

**Note:** *Names in this document have been changed to protect confidentiality.*

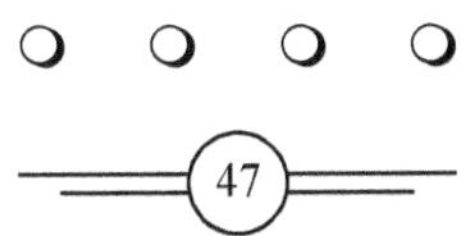

www.ingramcontent.com/pod-product-compliance
Lightning Source LLC
LaVergne TN
LVHW011604210726